## The museum itself is a work of art.

—Gio Ponti

SCALA

# Denver Art Museum

ART SPACES

## From the Director

The Denver Art Museum's expansion, named after board chairman Frederic C. Hamilton, allows us to display more of our outstanding collections. But more than that, this building embodies new experiences and ideas. With the opening of the Hamilton Building, we have a museum as visionary on the outside as it is on the inside.

As we found with our first major building, designed by Gio Ponti in the late 1960s, an innovative structure is not an end in itself; it is a catalyst. An exciting new building allows a museum to showcase better exhibitions and fosters increased attendance and collection growth. A new structure gives museum staff an opportunity to reevaluate the way art is presented, interpreted, and accessed. Daniel Libeskind's design for the Hamilton Building has not just pushed architectural boundaries, it has also challenged all of us—from construction workers to staff to museum visitors—to think differently.

Everyone involved has been a true partner in the realization of this building. It would not have been possible, of course, without the support of the people and the City of Denver. In its relatively short history,

> Museum director Lewis I. Sharp

Denver has evolved from a mining outpost to having the tenth-largest downtown in the country. The pioneer spirit that founded the city and the entrepreneurial energy that drove its tremendous growth is visible today in the groundbreaking collaborations—between government, citizens, private enterprise, and cultural institutions—that produced this incredible building.

Lewis I. Sharp
Frederick and Jan Mayer Director
Denver Art Museum

# Denver Art Museum:
# The North Building

Far from being a departure for the Denver Art Museum, the expansion designed by Daniel Libeskind continues a tradition of innovation. The Denver Art Museum's first significant building, now known as the North Building, was designed by the brilliant Italian architect Gio Ponti in collaboration with Denver architects James Sudler and Joal Cronenwett. Something of a celebrity in Europe, Ponti (1891–1979) isn't well known in America, primarily because the Denver Art Museum remains his only public building on the North American continent. His legacy looms large, however, and includes not just buildings but also flatware, theater costumes, office furniture, countless writings, and even the interior of an ocean liner.

Ponti remained in Italy for the duration of the North Building's design and construction. His major contribution was its exterior. He started with two towers, then sliced off the corners to create an irregular, twenty-four-sided form. The surface is covered with a combination of flat and pyramid-shaped tiles, which create subtle patterns when the sunlight strikes in just the right way. All along the building's crown, the roofline is enlivened by cut-out shapes that frame pieces of Denver's vibrantly blue sky. The young Daniel Libeskind, who read about the project in the early 1970s, was one of the building's early fans.

◄ The North Building

◄ "The window views
provide little escapes
into framed landscapes,"
wrote Gio Ponti.[2]

> The outline of the museum's crown is open to the sky, the beautiful Denver sky.[1]
> —Gio Ponti

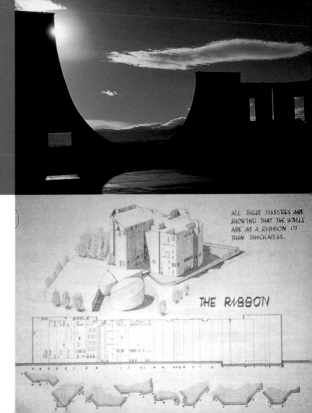

▲ Corning Glass Works manufactured more than a million tiles to cover the surface of the North Building. It took workers two years to set them all by hand.

➤ In order to visualize the North Building's exterior, the architects created drawings that "unfolded" the building's twenty-four sides and flattened them out into a long ribbon.

ALL THESE FISSURES ARE SHOWING THAT THE WALLS ARE AS A RIBBON OF THIN THICKNESS.

THE RIBBON

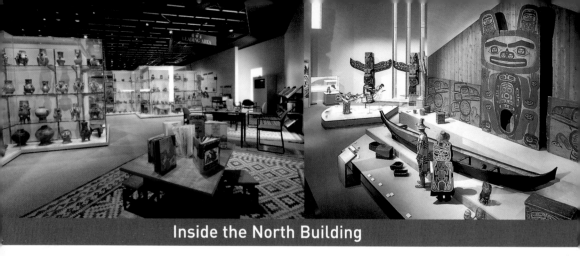

## Inside the North Building

Left to right:
the pre-Columbian study gallery, the Northwest Coast American Indian art gallery, the Discovery Library, and the building's lower level

Gio Ponti didn't determine the North Building's interior configuration—that was done by former museum director Otto Bach. Bach wanted a modern, vertical building that would be easy for visitors to navigate. Each of the two towers was designed to have no more than ten thousand square feet per floor—the amount of space Bach believed visitors could tour without experiencing "museum fatigue."

To provide the museum with the greatest flexibility, the galleries were conceived simply as white boxes for displaying art. Since the North Building's 1971 opening, the galleries have undergone several transformations. Today, visitors see the results of an extensive renovation that took place in the 1990s. The pre-Columbian spaces on the fourth floor, for example, now feature a study

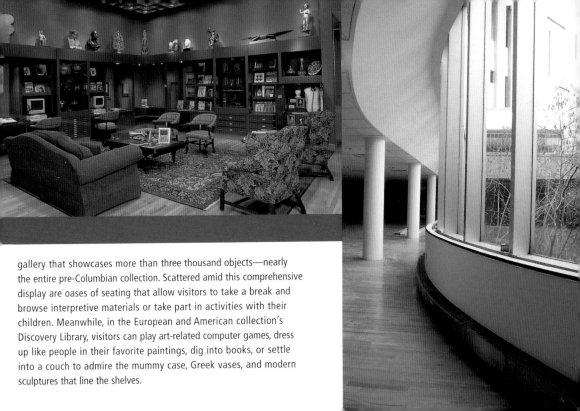

gallery that showcases more than three thousand objects—nearly the entire pre-Columbian collection. Scattered amid this comprehensive display are oases of seating that allow visitors to take a break and browse interpretive materials or take part in activities with their children. Meanwhile, in the European and American collection's Discovery Library, visitors can play art-related computer games, dress up like people in their favorite paintings, dig into books, or settle into a couch to admire the mummy case, Greek vases, and modern sculptures that line the shelves.

## Art & Experiences

Founded in 1893, the Denver Art Museum is the largest and most comprehensive art museum between Chicago and the West Coast. Its holdings include more than sixty thousand objects divided between eight curatorial departments: Architecture, Design, and Graphics; Asian Art; European and American Painting and Sculpture; Modern and Contemporary Art; Native Arts (including American Indian, African, and Oceanic art); Pre-Columbian and Spanish Colonial Art; Textile Art; and Western American Art.

The museum was one of the first to collect and display American Indian objects as art rather than cultural artifacts, and its American Indian collection remains among the finest anywhere. The museum's collections of pre-Columbian and Spanish colonial

> *The Things I Have to Do to Maintain Myself*, 1994, Roxanne Swentzell. Funds from Polly and Mark Addison.

objects are also remarkable, in terms of both range and artistic merit—the Spanish colonial collection is the most comprehensive in the country.

The museum also takes pride in its commitment to its visitors. Throughout the museum, comfortable corners stocked with videos, books, and picture-filled brochures beckon those seeking more information.

Art-based games, dress-up areas, and artmaking activities lure children and adventurous grownups. There are even touchable objects for those who ache to know what the art feels like. The museum strives to offer each person—whether adult or child, art historian or first-time visitor—opportunities to have meaningful experiences with the art.

▲ *Untitled (for A.C.)*, 1992, Dan Flavin. Funds from the NBT Foundation.

# Denver Art Museum:
# The Frederic C. Hamilton Building

Great design adds value to a city. It adds psychic value, aesthetic value, and economic value, because it says that you're a city that is moving, you're a city that is progressive, you're a city that has confidence in itself. I think Denver's ready for it.

—Jennifer Moulton, Director of Community Planning & Development for the City of Denver, 1991–2003

## Denver Decides to Build

> Civic Center Park and
downtown Denver

In early 1999, museum director Lewis Sharp and then-mayor Wellington Webb happened to meet at the museum's restaurant, which had become a favorite lunch spot for local politicians. Although these chance meetings happened frequently, the conversation that day would have a major impact on the museum's future. It had been obvious for years that too much of the museum's growing collection was in storage. Crowds clamoring to see exhibitions were overflowing the galleries, and the museum's renowned education programs were cramped for lack of space. Looking at the burgeoning local economy, Sharp and Webb decided that the time was right for the museum to expand.

With the blessing of the city, the museum sought a public bond to fund the expansion. Voters were promised not just a bigger museum but also an architectural landmark for the city of Denver. The museum's board of trustees committed to raising an additional $50 million endowment to maintain the new building. On November 2, 1999, Denver voters resoundingly approved a $62.5 million bond to pay for the construction of a new Denver Art Museum building.

# Imagining the Future

With the possibility for funding looking good, the museum's staff, trustees, and visitors sought to articulate their vision of the museum's future. A picture emerged of a museum complex that would celebrate its world-class collections, be a primary destination for major traveling exhibitions, and provide opportunities for rich, meaningful interactions with art.

By the end of their discussions, the museum stakeholders had produced documents that would serve as both an introduction and a road map for architectural candidates. The documents outlined the new building's needs: increased gallery space; strict control over temperature, humidity, and ultraviolet light; integrated high-tech security systems; and so on. But the lists also included less tangible and more ambitious desires: a grand entry space, an unparalleled spatial environment, a building of international architectural stature, and, in the end, a unified museum complex.

Our initial vision was to build the first great art museum of the twenty-first century. That's not just the bricks and mortar but also the program, the vision, and the way the building sits within the city.

—R. Craig Miller, Curator of Architecture, Design & Graphics, Denver Art Museum

## Finding the Architect

With its vision on paper, the museum set out to select an architect. Soon after the successful passage of the bond, architecture critic and author Victoria Newhouse helped a group of staff, including museum director Lewis Sharp, architecture curator R. Craig Miller, and modern and contemporary art curator Dianne Perry Vanderlip, compile a list of dream architects. The museum sent requests for qualifications to forty-one architects. Out of the nineteen who responded, the field was narrowed to ten, then to five, and finally to three: Arata Isozaki, Thom Mayne, and Daniel Libeskind. At the same time, the mayor appointed an

architect selection committee (consisting of city officials, cultural leaders, and Denver citizens) who worked with museum trustees to evaluate the candidates.

In June 2000, the three finalists traveled to Denver to take part in a public forum. Public interest overwhelmed capacity, and more than eight hundred people squeezed into a small lecture space in the Denver Public Library. A month later, the finalists returned, this time to conduct workshops with the selection committee. No designs were presented; the finalists were merely given information and asked to describe their approach to completing the task.

The Brain—is wider than the Sky—
For—put them side by side—
The one the other will contain
With ease—and You—beside—

—From an Emily Dickinson poem
Libeskind recited during his
final presentation

They were judged on their strategy as well as their ability to comprehend and respond to the unique needs of the museum.

In July 2000, the selection committee announced its choice. With his impossible-to-resist combination of enthusiasm, energy, and vision, Daniel Libeskind had captured the imagination of both the committee and the Denver community. The coup de grace was his final presentation, where, in his heavily accented, rapid-fire English, he interwove art, poetry, and a complex analysis of architectural history. "With every encounter, you knew that you were dealing with someone that was operating at a higher level," says Sharp.

I've had several different lifetimes.

—Daniel Libeskind

Daniel Libeskind was born in Poland in 1946, the son of two Holocaust survivors. He spent his formative years in Communist Poland, an environment he describes as "not really conducive to creativity." At the age of eleven, he immigrated to Israel with his parents, learned a new language, and habituated to a new culture. But two years later, the family set off again, this time for New York.

Libeskind was one of the last immigrants to arrive by boat through Ellis Island. "The most incredible experience is to see New York from there, from the water," he says. "As a true immigrant, you don't know anybody, you have no real connection, and yet you are part of that American history." Libeskind became an American citizen in 1965.

Long before he became an architect, Libeskind was a musical prodigy. While he was still a child, his performances on the accordion won international competitions and drew praise from such luminaries as the violinist Isaac Stern. He left music to study architecture at New York's Cooper Union for the Advancement of Science and Art. But after his post-graduate work at Essex University in England, Libeskind

worked as a professor and theorist. He didn't complete his first commission, Berlin's Jewish Museum, until he was fifty-two. It was worth the wait. The Jewish Museum was a resounding success: without a single object on view, the empty museum drew almost 350,000 visitors. It was while working in Berlin that Libeskind received the Denver Art Museum's request for qualifications.

The DAM chose Libeskind more than two years before he would be tapped as the master plan architect for the World Trade Center site in New York City and catapulted to a level of celebrity that few architects achieve. In the summer of 2000, Libeskind had completed only two buildings, both in Germany and both museums: the Jewish Museum in Berlin and the Felix Nussbaum Haus in Osnabrück.

While Libeskind's highly theoretical designs challenge traditional notions of space, his pragmatism keeps him grounded. "What I've realized," says Nina Libeskind, his wife and business partner, "is that his brilliance lies not just in his ability to conceive of unusual buildings and unusual spaces, but to get them built."

WORLD

CONFLICT

SHARDS OF THE GLOBE

MUSEUM

Concept sketch and photograph of the Imperial War Museum North in Manchester, England

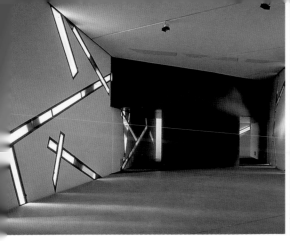

You cannot see his buildings in photographs and understand his buildings completely, because they are as much about how you feel in the buildings as how you see.

—Jennifer Moulton, Director of Community Planning & Development for the City of Denver, 1991–2003

▲ Interior and exterior views of the Jewish Museum in Berlin

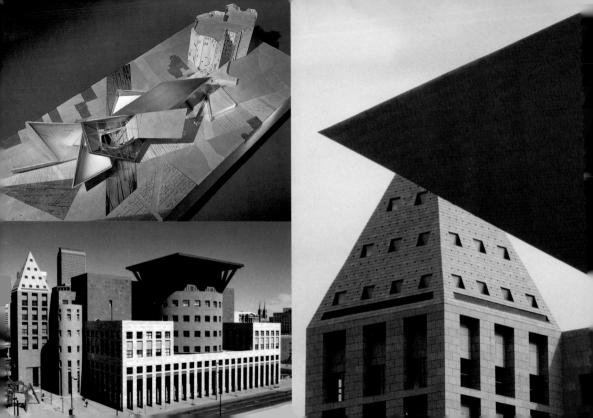

## The Early Concept

Less than a month after his selection, Libeskind formed a joint venture with Denver-based Davis Partnership Architects and began work on his design concept. From the start, Libeskind knew that the expansion would need to relate to the museum's North Building—no easy job, given Gio Ponti's idiosyncratic design. But the expansion building would also be seen in the context of its closest neighbor to the northeast, the Denver Public Library. In 1995, superstar architect Michael Graves completed an expansion of the library's original building. With its striking geometric shapes, bold colors, and imposing size, the library is one of the most recognizable buildings in downtown Denver.

As he thought about the site, Libeskind conceived of a nexus: a building that would link the museum and the library and also be a bridge between downtown Denver and the residential neighborhood to the south. He wanted a structure that would not function merely as an addition but would unify the site into a new complex.

But how to do this? Libeskind ruminated on one of his favorite works of art, Michelangelo's *Creation of Adam*, on the ceiling of the Sistine Chapel. He mulled over the famous gesture between God and Adam, the idea of "those two fingers, meeting in that space that doesn't quite touch." He thought about a structure that could forge connections by reaching toward the North Building, the library, and all of downtown.

◀ Top left, a 2002 model built by Davis Partnership Architects shows the Hamilton Building reaching toward the North Building.

◀ Bottom and right, the Denver Public Library

> ## Where else but in Denver could you build something so bold?
>
> —Daniel Libeskind

ʌ An early concept watercolor by Daniel Libeskind, 2000

◄ Downtown Denver against the Rocky Mountains

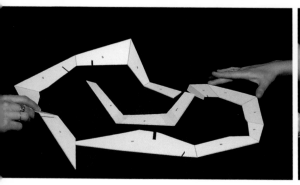
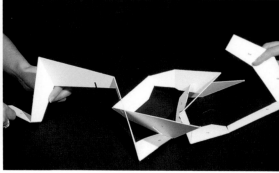

## Inspiration in Three Dimensions

When asked about his inspiration for the
Hamilton Building, Libeskind always gives
the same answer: Denver. "I never tire of
saying it," he asserts. "This building is not
transplanted from another place, it couldn't
be anywhere else." The building's basic
shape came to him when he saw the Rocky

Mountains from the window of an airplane.
"I sketched them on the back of my boarding
pass, and when that was filled, on the back of
the in-flight magazine."[3]

Rob Claiborne, former project architect
for Studio Daniel Libeskind, remembers that
sketch: "It was a very simple sketch of space

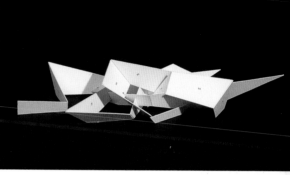

made up of two lines, and in the seed of those two lines was everything necessary to create an incredible space for art."

With this initial sketch as a foundation, Studio Libeskind architects imagined what these two lines would look like in three dimensions. They improvised an unusual working method that Claiborne describes as "a spatial dance." With Libeskind directing, two architects each took a long strip of paper. "Working opposite each other, we folded, joined, and moved these strips," Claiborne explains. At the end of the process, the team had its first 3-D design.

⌃ To take his early sketches into the third dimension, Libeskind and his team experimented by folding long strips of paper.

## The Building Evolves

For many projects, architectural models are made solely for the client's benefit; for the Denver Art Museum expansion, models helped the architects visualize the unprecedented spaces they were creating. Libeskind's team and their local counterparts at Davis Partnership Architects created more than two hundred models—including a scale model large enough for the architects to stick their heads into.

With each new model, the design evolved. Libeskind's original concept of an underground connection to the North Building could not be realized due to the budget and the difficulty of navigating around the utility lines beneath the street. But most design changes resulted from the collaboration between Libeskind's team and museum staff. The galleries initially reserved for the museum's collections were later designated as temporary exhibition spaces in order to keep the collections in the expansion closer to the collections remaining in the North Building. Windows were made smaller or eliminated in places where artwork needed to be protected from too much light. Other adjustments were made to meet the museum's unique security, cleanliness, temperature, and humidity requirements.

Aware of the necessity of evolution, Libeskind focuses on maintaining the creative momentum of his projects. "This design concept is just as strong, if not stronger, than the original concepts proffered at the time of the design," says Brit Probst, principal architect of Davis Partnership Architects. "That's incredibly unusual."

◄ The architects created more than two hundred models of the Hamilton Building, including this one, built by Davis Partnership.

I wouldn't call them changes. It's an evolution . . . Just as the sketch becomes a building, the design undergoes an organic transformation.

—Daniel Libeskind

## An Interview with Daniel Libeskind

Q: There are many different places from which you can view the building. How do you feel about all those different perspectives?

It's a building that changes with almost every footstep you take—no, not almost—with every inch of your movement. With every millimeter shift of your iris, the building changes, and that was the idea. Denver's a dynamic place, the people are dynamic. It's not a sleepy place, it's not a place that has been; it's a place always of the future. And that is part of the composition of the building. People complete the building. It is not an autonomous entity, ready and finished and closed, but it depends on every single perspective to make it alive. That's what the building's actually designed for, is to be completed: by the dynamic experience of the passerby, or the visitor, or somebody driving by in the car, or even somebody looking at the building from a workplace in the downtown. The function of architecture is not just to add another building but to transform the environment so that it is a better place to be, a more interesting place to be, more stimulating and also more poetic.

**Q: You've talked about the atrium model that was created on an exceptionally large scale. Why did you have it built on such a large scale?**

I think ultimately you have to be able to look at the space in a direct relationship to your eye and to your body. You can't just see it in a rendering or in a drawing, because it is meant to be looked at from dynamic points of view. No advanced computer technology, no simulation can ever replace your head just moving around, looking at the light, and feeling. Ultimately architecture is not about knowing the things you've studied about or been told about in a newspaper or in a book. It's a feeling.

**Q: So you were very physically engaged with the atrium models?**

The funniest story with the atrium, I have to say, was when I first started working with the building, and the Denver Art Museum team visited me. My office at that time was still in Berlin, and we had an atrium model on a piece of glass. I'll never forget, I was so shocked—there was the director of the museum, Lewis Sharp, lying on the floor, with his back on the floor, looking up. I said, *this* is a person who understands architecture. Architecture is not a two-dimensional art, it's not something you just photograph—it's something that you really have to walk around, feel. And feel it not just with your brain, but feel it with your ankles, with your feet, with your whole body, and enjoy it. And I think that's really how the atrium was designed. It was designed as something that will affect every dimension of your body. It's not just something abstract.

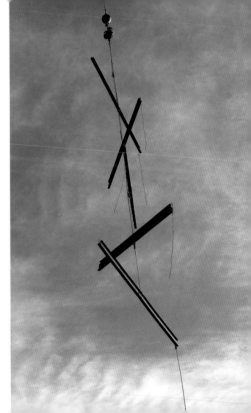

Q: What was the hardest part of developing the atrium?

The most complex part was how to reconcile the different programmatic needs for the atrium—where is there gallery space, where is there light, where is there an atmosphere of solitude, where is there a public celebratory atmosphere—and to incorporate it all in a single space. I use the word overture. When you listen to Mozart's Requiem, the first few bars—I think the twenty-three first bars—incorporate an entire lengthy work. The atrium really is an introduction in many ways. I think the qualities that you can discover there will be verified by your experience in the museum. The first sounds, the atmosphere, the connectivity with that atmosphere—the mood is set. And I think it's proper that an atrium should set those moods because that's where you quite literally enter, get informed, get ready for an adventure with art.

Q: Did you know early on that you would use titanium cladding, or was it a large search and a painstaking process?

We had an aim from the very beginning: a building that is luminous, that has subtlety in it, a building that reflects a variety of conditions both at night and during the day, and a building that will never be an inert abstraction on the landscape but something that is really vitally part of the surrounding natural landscape and beautiful crystalline shape of the downtown. But to find the material, and to be able to actually achieve this in practice, is also a matter of good luck. And we did have good luck that we were able to use titanium, which I would say is the ideal material for this building. As you walk by it, as you touch it, as you see it from distant perspectives, it has the luminosity of light itself. There's a magic in it, and I think that is part of the right quality for this building.

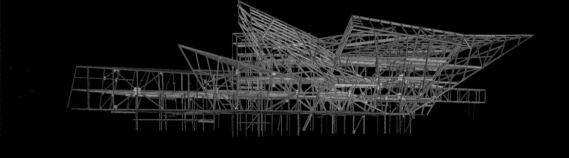

## Technology

▲ Virtual model of the
building's steel structure

From its low-tech beginnings—sketches on
hotel notepads, folded strips of paper, card-
board models—the Denver Art Museum
expansion rapidly evolved into a construction
and engineering tour de force that would
have been nearly impossible to build even
ten years earlier. Technology was so pervasive

during the project that even the design of
the scaffolding was done on computers.

The contractor, M. A. Mortenson
Company, was brought on board to solve
construction challenges even before the
design was complete. Architects converted
physical models into virtual ones, which

were given to the engineers and contractors. Because architects and engineers used compatible technology to plan the building's systems (like the plumbing, ductwork, and electrical components), Mortenson could easily merge their designs to see possible coordination problems before they happened.

Technology enabled hundreds of issues to be resolved prior to construction and saved an immeasurable amount of money and time. Nearly all of the joints that connect the steel beams were custom-made to suit the building's unique angles. When the time came to build, Mortenson already knew how and where each beam connected—as well as the size and quantity of bolts necessary to complete each connection. Each of the massive beams was set in place using an electronic tracking system and spatial coordinates. The steel beams were tagged, and digital survey equipment honed in on the reflective stickers several times a day to make sure that each beam was positioned correctly.

# Construction

In July 2003, ground was broken and construction began.

Steel construction started simply, with the only truly vertical beams in the building: the emergency exit stairwells and elevator shafts. Next came the relatively orthogonal part of the structure to the south, which houses the temporary exhibition galleries. Work progressed northward and ended with the most complex part of the structure, the hundred-foot prow that cantilevers over Thirteenth Avenue. The painstaking process of mapping the placement of each beam and bolt prior to construction paid off when the steel frame was completed ahead of schedule.

◄ Groundbreaking

We had an aim from the very beginning: a building that is luminous, that has subtlety in it, a building that reflects a variety of conditions both at night and during the day, and a building that will never be an inert abstraction on the landscape.

—Daniel Libeskind

## Titanium

For the building's outermost layer, Libeskind chose titanium: nine thousand panels in all, each about seven feet wide by twenty inches high. "It's almost like fabric," he rhapsodizes. And indeed, because the panels are less reflective than many other metals, the building's surface can appear almost soft, despite the fact that titanium is as strong as steel. This lack of reflectivity is both aesthetic and practical: instead of glinting dangerously in the sun, the titanium changes color with the light of the sky. Furthermore, as Libeskind explains, the hue and texture of the panels complements the gray glass tiles that cover the museum's North Building. The panels are also lightweight, resist corrosion, and are easy to clean. In addition, titanium was the perfect choice of material for Denver, which is home to the country's largest titanium producer.

# Engineering the Impossible

What makes the Hamilton Building most visibly different from other buildings are its exterior walls, almost all of which lean outward. To enable the building to stand on its own, the tremendous weight of these leaning walls has to be transferred through the building's central core and foundation deep into bedrock. The steel frame connects to a concrete foundation, which includes 116 reinforced concrete pillars that extend more than sixty-five feet below ground into solid rock.

Until the steel frame was completely assembled, however, it couldn't even hold itself upright. As the steel skeleton took shape, it was supported by temporary bracing called shoring towers. Sixty-two towers—some more than seventy feet high—were used during construction. Pressure sensors measured the amount of weight on each tower and allowed the contractor, M. A. Mortenson Company, to determine when each tower could be safely removed.

➤ "The most unique thing about the steel framing is the amount of temporary bracing and shoring required to hold the frame up," says Dave Sandlin, construction executive at M. A. Mortenson Company. "The building's like a giant truss—until it's fully together, it's not holding itself up."

No one person can build a building.

—Daniel Libeskind

Inside the building labels: African, Modern & Contemporary, Atrium, Oceanic, Modern & Contemporary, Special Exhibitions, Special Exhibitions, Western, Special Exhibitions, Museum Shop, Lobby, Cafe, Art Storage, Auditorium, Art Storage

# Inside the Hamilton Building

The DAM asked Daniel Libeskind for a museum with large interior spaces, high ceilings, and interesting architectural features. The museum's staff further delineated the interior by specifying the placement of the walls that shape the galleries, hold art, and guide visitors.

"Daniel Libeskind developed the sculptural shape of the building," explains Dan Kohl, Director of Museum Design. Kohl's job was the inside of the building, making sure the museum's "program"—art, education, security, visitor amenities, and so on—would fit in this sculptural form. Kohl started out by ensuring the building would be "if not immediately intuitive, at least easy to navigate over time." To help visitors keep their bearings, the galleries are organized around a central core: a grand staircase that winds through the atrium up to the fourth floor. Bathrooms are located in the same place on each floor, both to help visitors find them easily and guarantee that, in the unlikely event of a plumbing problem, they'll only leak on top of each other.

◄ Location of galleries in
the Hamilton Building

► The DAM's Director
of Museum Design,
Dan Kohl (left), looks
at a gallery model with
Daniel Libeskind.

"The work of art is not performed by the artist alone. The viewer completes the art." Marcel Duchamp

As for the galleries, Kohl and the DAM's exhibition designers approached each space individually, with an eye for the artwork, the visitor experiences, and the atmosphere in each area. Their desire "not to deny the architecture" was a major challenge. "We tried to find solutions that celebrate the art as well as give the architecture its space and voice," Kohl says. Kohl's close collaboration with Libeskind enabled him to get a handle on the architect's visual language. "There's an internal consistency to his geometry; it takes a little while to understand," Kohl explains. "By understanding Daniel's intentions, if I want to borrow from his geometry, at least I know what the rulebook is." Kohl put these ideas to work in the interior spaces. "Daniel created the melody, and our exhibition design was essentially an improv, a riff on that melody," he says.

‹ *Quantum Cloud XXXIII*, 2000, Antony Gormley. Funds in honor of Lewis I. Sharp from the NBT Foundation.

› Model of the third-floor modern and contemporary galleries

For thirty years, the Modern and Contemporary Art Department didn't have a permanent gallery space in the museum. Nevertheless, founding curator Dianne Perry Vanderlip amassed a collection of more than six thousand objects, including one of the country's largest holdings of Robert Motherwell paintings, an impressive collection of photography, and the world's largest archive of work by Bauhaus artist Herbert Bayer. The DAM was the first art museum in the United States to purchase works by Damien Hirst, Sean Scully, Neo Rauch, and many other artists.

The collection finally came into its own with two new floors of gallery space in the Hamilton Building. The design of the department's first permanent galleries started with the art. "We had to take the

collection apart and put it into groupings—pop art, conceptual art, minimalism—that would relate and look good together," says Vanderlip, the DAM's Polly and Mark Addison Curator of Modern and Contemporary Art. After basic groupings had been established, the team thought about where to place the walls.

Libeskind's architecture created some inspired locations for art. The top-floor gallery, for example, features one of the most extraordinary spaces in the Hamilton Building. Two outward-leaning walls meet at a dramatic angle that extends more than thirty feet in the air. (From outside the building, a viewer would see this as the building's "prow," which juts out over Thirteenth Avenue.) Vanderlip chose this as the location for Antony Gormley's large steel sculpture *Quantum Cloud XXXIII* and positioned lights from below to cast the sculpture's shadow across the sloping walls.

▲ In addition to the works by Vasa (Velizar Mihich), Gene Davis, and Richard Anuszkiewicz shown in the model above, the fourth-floor modern and contemporary art galleries feature sculptures by Dan Flavin, Robert Irwin, Richard Serra, and Robert Smithson.

*Tan Warm* and *Tan Cool* © Richard Anuszkiewicz/Licensed by VAGA, New York, NY.

# Western American Art Galleries

Reinforcing the DAM's dedication to celebrating Denver's heritage and to exhibiting a broad view of the art of the American West, the western collection's permanent galleries opened on the seventh floor of the North Building in the late 1990s. In 2001, several major gifts of art spurred the creation of the Institute of Western American Art and launched a new era for the collection. Today, the prominent placement of the western American art galleries on the second floor of the Hamilton Building announces the museum's firm commitment to the art of this region.

At the heart of the western galleries is a long thoroughfare that divides the space in half. Exhibition designers established this axis—which stretches from the door of the western galleries across the bridge that connects the museum's two buildings—to help visitors orient themselves in Libeskind's unusual spaces. Anticipating heavy traffic between the buildings, the exhibition team planned this "main street" as a place for eye-catching art, where unexpected modern works sit beside historic monuments of western art.

To either side of this axis, individual gallery spaces beckon visitors to stray from the primary path. Rather than choosing a thematic or chronological arrangement, the western team arranged the galleries around different ways of experiencing artwork. In the gallery designed especially for contemplation, there is no explanatory wall text. Instead, seating is combined with scattered journals and stations that let visitors choose from a selection of music. Other areas focus on a single work of art, which visitors can explore with the help of videos, picture-filled brochures, and cards with the artist's responses to frequently asked questions. A more traditional museum gallery with wall text allows curators to show rarely seen or light-sensitive artwork on a rotating basis.

▶ *In the Enemy's Country*, 1921, Charles Marion Russell. Gift of the Magness family in memory of Betsy Magness.

▲ *The Cheyenne*, 1901, Frederic Remington. Funds from William D. Hewit Charitable Annuity Trust.

◄ Model of the western American art galleries

# African & Oceanic Art Galleries

Both the African and the Oceanic collections are unique among art museums. Curator Moyo Okediji has made a point of adding contemporary art to both collections. "Contemporary artists express the changes that are redefining indigenous cultures," he explains. "After seeing both old and recent pieces, visitors start to enjoy the dynamic nature of culture."

The Denver Art Museum's African art collection is the most comprehensive in the Rocky Mountain region and features works of art from every part of Africa. But when the first visitors stepped into the Hamilton Building's African galleries, it had been nearly a decade since most of the art had been on public view.

African art hasn't always worked well within traditional museums, most of which were created to suit European and American ideas about art. In African cultures, art is used in everyday life, not put on a pedestal. The African collection's exhibition team wanted a space that would give viewers a better feel for what the art would look like in its original contexts—worn in whirling dances, glimpsed by firelight during ceremonies, or handled during day-to-day life.

Director of Museum Design Dan Kohl and exhibition designer Lehlan Murray decided against a traditional gallery arrangement, in which art is installed along the gallery's perimeter walls. Instead, they created an irregular landscape of platforms in the center of the space. As visitors walk through this landscape, they get fragmentary glimpses and oblique views of the artwork. "In a sense we have a gallery without walls," Okediji says, "which works so very well with African art because in Africa, the galleries have no walls. Art is found in markets, in the community, in quiet groves."

The museum chose a small but dramatic space directly below the African galleries for the Oceanic collection, which comprises objects from South Pacific cultures. Here, Kohl designed a series of freestanding cases as metaphors for the islands of the South Pacific. Each case is extra tall to make sure visitors have a seamless view of the objects, while wave forms on the protective glass recall the objects' ocean-side origins.

Model of the fourth-floor African galleries

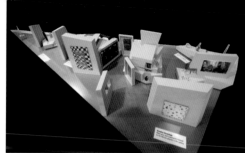

Malagan Fish Figure, date unknown, New Ireland, Papua New Guinea. Gift of Joan and George Anderman.

Ere Egungun Masquerade, 1950s, Yoruba, Nigeria. Native arts acquisition funds and partial gift of Michael and Patricia Coronel.

◄ Libeskind designed the housing, office, and retail space that surrounds the parking garage.

## An Urban Neighborhood Takes Shape

From the beginning, it was clear that the Denver Art Museum expansion would have a galvanizing effect on the city. Even the building's parking structure turned into a unique opportunity.

Because the Hamilton Building was built on the museum's old parking lot, the city required the museum to add a parking garage. The initial idea of underground parking was ruled out because of the cost. Faced with the inevitable prospect of a five-story garage across the street from the museum, Libeskind and Denver city planner Jennifer Moulton turned what could have been a negative into a positive. "Here was an opportunity to create an urban space,"

Libeskind says, "and it occurred to me that the most beautiful thing would be to have people living there." Libeskind and Moulton proposed "wrapping" the parking structure on three sides with housing, offices, and retail space.

An innovative partnership between the museum, the City of Denver, and a private developer made the plan happen. Libeskind designed all of the buildings, including fifty-six condominiums that look out onto the Hamilton Building. The street that had separated the two sites was permanently closed to create a pedestrian plaza where the museum could host outdoor programs.

It doesn't end when it's finished being built—it begins its life.

—Daniel Libeskind

# Facts & Figures

Through a process begun in 1999, the Denver Art Museum produced one of the most complicated architectural structures in the world. The Hamilton Building is the result of:

- 10 public forums, hosting more than 6,000 citizens

- $62.5 million in voter-approved bond funds

- 3 countries visited to explore buildings by contending architects

- About 150,000 air miles logged between Berlin and Denver during the design process

- The support of 2 City of Denver administrations

- The efforts of more than 200 museum staff members

- More than 30 subcontractors working for 3 years

- 1 architect sharing his dream with a city

Size of the Hamilton Building = 146,000 square feet, including about 55,000 square feet of display space

Size of the total Denver Art Museum complex = 356,000 square feet

Tons of steel used in the Hamilton Building = 2,750 (3 times the amount that would be used in a conventional building of the same size)

Steel bolts = 50,000

Shoring towers used to prop up the steel skeleton during construction = 62

Titanium panels covering the building's surface = 9,000

Reinforced cement piers that ground the building = 116, each reaching 65 feet underground

Construction workers enjoyed Denver's driest March since 1908, battled the wettest June since 1966, and endured the 4th-warmest July since 1872.

Text by Laura Caruso and
Andrea Kalivas Fulton
Design by Pooja Bakri and Shar Huston
Edited by Deanna Lee and Lisa Levinson

## Endnotes

Except when identified below, quotations
are taken from interviews conducted by the
museum. Portions of some of these interviews
can be found in the videos *Selection of the
Architect, Spatial Dance*, and *The Frederic C.
Hamilton Building Takes Shape*, all directed
and produced by Amie Knox and Jocelyn
Childs (Denver: A bar K Productions).
To purchase, visit the Museum Shop at
www.denverartmuseum.org, or call
720.865.5035.

title page: Douglas Davis, "The Museum
Explosion," *Newsweek*, September 17, 1973, 89.
1. Gio Ponti, "In Denver," *Domus* 511 (June
1972): 1.
2. Esther McCoy, "Architecture West,"
*Progressive Architecture*, February 1972, 46.
3. Daniel Libeskind, *Breaking Ground:
Adventures in Life and Architecture*, with
Sarah Crichton (New York: Riverhead Books,
2004), 8.

## Photography Credits

Except when noted below, photographs and
assistance courtesy of the Denver Art Museum's
Photographic Services Department, including but
not limited to: Dan Ferguson, Hans Hansen, Kevin
Hester, Jan Melson, William O'Connor, Winter
Prather, Lloyd Rule, Eric Stephenson, Carole Lee
Vowell, and Jeff Wells.
Drawing on p. 7, The Gio Ponti Archive, Denver;
pp. 12, 16, and 33, Dan Kohl; photos on pp.
22–23, © bitterbredt.de and ROM; concept
sketch on p. 22, © Daniel Libeskind; photo of
Denver Public Library on bottom left of p. 24,
Rhoda Pollack; photo on p. 26, Bob Ashe for the
Denver Metro Convention and Visitors Bureau;
pp. 28–29, © Studio Daniel Libeskind with Davis
Partnership, a joint venture; p. 36, courtesy of
Dowco Consultants Ltd. in Xsteel; p. 44, rendering
by Miller Hare and Davis Partnership Architects;
sculpture on p. 46, © courtesy of the artist and
Jay Jopling/White Cube; p. 53, © Studio Daniel
Libeskind with Davis Partnership, a joint venture,
courtesy of Mile High Development and Corporex
Colorado; p. 55, courtesy David Baysinger, Denver
Museum of Nature and Science.

Printed and bound in China
10 9 8 7 6 5 4 3 2 1

Published by Scala Publishers Ltd
10 Northburgh Street
London EC1V 0AT, UK
www.scalapublishers.com
in association with the Denver Art Museum.
Distributed outside the DAM in the
book trade by Antique Collectors' Club
Ltd, Eastworks, 116 Pleasant St, Suite
#60B, Easthampton, MA 01027, USA.

ISBN: 1-85759-431-2
Library of Congress Control Number:
2006903051

Denver Art Museum
100 West 14th Avenue Parkway
Denver, Colorado 80204
www.denverartmuseum.org